How To Find The Peace In You

How To Find The Peace In You

A Proven Way To Develop Great Behaviors

Eric Davis

Published by Tablo

Published in 2021 by Tablo Publishing.

Publisher and wholesale enquiries: orders@tablo.io

20 21 22 23 LSC 10 9 8 7 6 5 4 3 2 1

TABLE OF CONTENTS

DISCLAIMER

This book has been written for informational purposes only. Every effort has been made to make this book as complete and accurate as possible. The purpose of this book is to educate and inspire. The author and the publisher shall have neither liability or responsibility to any person or enmity with respect to any loss or damage caused or alleged to be caused directly or indirectly by this book.

INTRODUCTION

By the time we are adults, most of us will be skilled to be a form of ourselves that satisfies others. Regardless if it comes from the way we were constructed or how we were educated in school, we generally learn to cover up our flaws and become unsure of our very desires in life.

Sadly, that mentality won't lead us to be content and live an accomplished life. We can reveal the best version of ourselves and modify our lives so that we are no longer misled in our lives. We can select the life that was designed for ourselves.

In this book, we will have to devote ourselves to exam ourselves, aim to be mindful of our behaviors, and be frank with ourselves. This book is for us, and no one other than ourselves can know what we desire.

With devotion, exposure, and self-interest, we will be able to be the best versions of ourselves and finally expose our flaws that we held for so long. Are we really ready to declare our purpose and peace that is within ourselves?

Then let's start to examine our present lives and see how much we are currently our true self. My goal is to help people see themselves as a part of a bigger picture and know that true peace begins by leading ourselves. My method is to share the knowledge of God, and His strongest podium, myself.

ACCEPT OUR OWN

The best version of ourselves is being able to accept our own, but what does that mean? It's sometimes harder to explain things by recognizing what it is. With that being acknowledged, here's a list of what is accepting our own:

1. Stop satisfying others.
2. Stop hurting our own minds by damaging our temples.
3. Stop forcing ourselves to do something out of survival.
4. Stop being hard on ourselves.
5. Stop **judging others** and comparing ourselves.
6. Stop being a victim of our environment.
7. Stop acting in a way that pleases social media and not ourselves.

Accepting our own means that we operate in a God frequency and transfer our energy with our faith systems, worth, and essentially, what feels natural to us: godliness. When there is an adjustment with our inner peace (states of mind and aspirations) and outer magnetism (connection and relations) we are accepting our own minds.

"Acknowledging Ourselves". Have we ever felt like we are our attitude and the way that we hold ourselves diverse depending on who's around us and our environment?

We attend to play a deviate role when we're with people that we want to please or want to make sure they like us. As an example, we might operate entirely otherwise if we are at work with people we just met and want to befriend them. We tend to be ourselves when we are at home or with family. That is when we loosen up and become more vulnerable and less bothered about how others might classify us.

Common questions that stay in our minds every day are; "Am I happy in my career?", "Do I really understand my partner?", "Does my family really support me?", "Can I say no to my friends and they accept me?", "Do I like spending time more with myself than with friends?" The goal is to accept our own self in all walks of our life. Think critically, think independently, and think for ourselves.

HANGING UP BAD HABITS

Some of the questions in Chapter 1 could be testing us. An example could be "Do I like spending time more with myself than with friends?" If it's challenging to spend more time with your own self, rather than with friends, how can you truly be the best form of yourself? Being honest is a major practice that we make in life that keeps us on the surface with God.

It takes a long time to perceive that the private world is a habitual practice that is happening publicly. Since the private world is a pure reflection of us, it could give us a lot of knowledge about ourselves when we take the time to recognize and be mindful. Some of our habits are damaging our minds and even bodies. It could be an everyday smoking habit or even spending too much time with people who don't meet our best interests. We should never spend our present time with a person who does not have a future with us.

Do not forget about the **"outer me"** as well as the inner me in this present life. As an example, if you love your career, it can be a sign that you actually acknowledge your skills and abilities. You are able to clearly see what you're capable of and therefore not settling for careers that you don't like. It is that you are creating your own comfort.

Take a minute to list some of the things that you like in your community. That can be the way your intimate partner loves you, the way your friends make you feel about yourself or your personal life.

If I could change anything about my life, it would be the following:

1. How I let people control me
2. My incapbility of not accepting
3. How I can't control my emotions
4. Jeaulsy
5. How I depend on others for my happiness

Now that you have recorded a few things you'd like to change about your life. Let us manifest what that means in relation to yourself. Am
I always going to forget about my needs and please others? Do I have a hard time putting myself first? Am I able to recognize my skills and abilities? Am I hard on myself, am I good enough?

What if the answers to these questions were, “I believe I could be loved for being myself, therefore I don't have to act like another person to gain love”. What have we learned about ourselves in that exercise? Are there aspects of us that we want to develop? Are these some habits that we would like to address and end our life span?

Next chapter, we will look at things that make us aware. Awareness is often another aspect that needs our activity. When we learn what sparks us, we learn about our true inner self and what needs to restore us within to be the best of our abilities. Prosperity is the consequence of our relentless, devotion, and development to a process.

DEVELOPING OUR SPARK

Are there some subjects that we avoid speaking with others because we know we'll get upset or discouraged? Do we sometimes find ourselves easily offended by others? Developing our spark will help us move from being conscious to being *at peace* with what others think when it's diverse from our opinion.

When we are sparked by something internal to us, we normally accuse others for what we are experiencing. Accusing others for our mindset and situations is deceiving ourselves. The quicker we can learn to stop reacting to others; the quicker our mindset will shift to be more in frequency with our true inner self.

We have to accept that the only thing we could change in this life is our attitude, our mentality, and our intelligence. As we know, we have no control over other people's attitude or mind. Make a choice now that we will no longer accuse our problems of outside circumstances.

Learn to be aware of our attitudes and understanding, especially when we go into the pattern of accusing others or acknowledging what they do or say. Start by making notes of what we feel sparks us.

Some examples can be government, social justice, inadequacy, etc. Strive to be as specific as possible by using examples to explain the sparks.

I normally respond passionately to the following:

- when I don't get what I want
- No validation
- when I can't control a situation
- When I can't read people
- Ignorince

Now make a strategy to respond differently in the future when those situations arise. How will we better handle our emotions in these situations? Another approach to this will be to understand why we get so compassionate to those situations. For example, for someone dating, they could feel like "it is always about the woman in my life". When are you going to understand that "I am important as well, and I deserve the same as others, if more"?

What sparks us, and when we explore this more thoroughly, what does it fulfill in our outside reality? Being the best form of ourselves means that we are breaking the shadows that have been haunting us, sometimes for years. Sometimes it's challenging, but when we face our dark side, we bring light and immediately allow ourselves to shine brighter than ever. It gives us the space to cure deep damages.

Taking control of our own peace of mind starts by acknowledging our importance in our own life and stops giving our power to others. When we accuse others for our faults, we don't own our control in our life. We are allowing others to rule our behavior and state of mind.

When we could maintain a fresh state of mind and stop the bad habits of responding to everything, we **become more at peace** within us and we could correctly exercise our energy and manifest our power which is God.

Next chapter, we will explore our roadblocks and how we could modify them to be more empowering. Those roadblocks are often connected to damages from the past that we carry with us for years.

DRIVING THROUGH OUR ROADBLOCKS

There are numerous reasons why someone wouldn't want to be there self completely. There are many experiences that create roadblocks to be our true selves. These roadblocks are damages such as neglect, dismissal, bias, shame, and dishonesty.

As a child, did we ever feel that we weren't needed? Do we feel nervous before we go on trips, facing a change in our life? Do we always need company around us? Do we easily give up a program or a goal along the way? Now that we can see and understand the obstacles that are damaging our mindset, we can now build solutions.

Shame

Shame is a profound damage because the one who suffers from it feels unfavorable in his/her existence. Therefore, it's almost impossible to be yourself when you carry that damage. It's not usual for people who feel ashamed to have a runaway mentality, that's to say, a body or part of the mind that seems to want to annoy or become very narrow-minded.

In terms of attitude, they are often confused about their right to exist. They seek isolation because if they accept a lot of attention, they would be afraid of not knowing what to do. They could be running, which is why they suggest not to attach themselves with material things because that will be restricting them from running. They often wonder what on Earth they are doing and find it hard to believe that they can be content here, while bringing something to the universe that's not astonishing.

Bias

The damage related to bias is intimately linked to the damage of shame. While shame deals deeply with "existing", the damage of bias is dealing with acquiring and existing. People who have the damage often have a firm mind, and are superb as possible. They have a graceful mind; firm movements; and very complex.

They're usually out-going people with powerful movements, but who are firm and lack adaptability. Often an overachiever and greedy. Those people tend to cut themselves off from their emotions and often cross their arms. They strive to be impeccable and justify themselves a lot. They find it hard to admit their issues. They often doubt their decisions. They like power and tend to control themselves by demanding a lot from others. They could be angry and upset, while struggling to show any passion. They do not want to be late but will often be postponed because they spend a long time preparing.

It's often challenging for people with the damage of bias to accept admiration, assistance, or offerings from others because they feel in debt toward the person afterward. The greatest fear of them is when others are insensitive to them because that awakens the favoritism and is also an observation of their shadow.

The initial step to heal our damages is to observe ourselves when we feel hurt. That could move on to accepting that we are not perfect, it is okay to embrace hurt. Last is to admit our fear and allow ourselves to move through the fear by being exposed and honest with ourselves by testing that fear.

PRODUCE NO LIMIT

Limits are the most underused ways to be the best versions of ourselves. Hip-Hop artist and entrepreneur Percy Miller (known as his rap name Master P), started his hip-hop career with his own record label named "No Limit", which produced many other artists and became one of the biggest major record labels to ever exist. One aspect of producing our own foundation is how we behave in our community; success often starts with the support of one's community before it expands. We must be clear about individuals who are encouraging and motivating us. We have to surround ourselves with people who admire us for who we truly are. Now is the perfect time to determine our true friends, communities and set goals around those who support us. Once we could recognize how we feel about the community we currently live in, we could then *build better values of our own life.* When Master P started No Limit records, he first started in his own community going neighborhood to neighborhood and later expanded all over the country. Restoring our own communities and minds are ***keys to power*;** **we have no limits on what we can do to improve our situations.**

INCREASING FAITH AND SELF-RESPECT

Faith is mostly attitude-based, and it's about knowing what our abilities are, while self-respect is more mentally, based on how we recognize ourselves. Faith and self-respect aren't always confident. An example could be how we could be great at something and trust our skill set (faith) but still view ourselves as losers (low self-respect). First, let's analyze faith and assess how strong our faith is.

Faith

Faith is about believing in our abilities and also our own understanding in choices. People with no faith will judge themselves by their actions or what they're incapable of achieving. When we experience no faith, we are likely to see the divisions in ourselves. Here are some questions that would help us assess our faith:

- Do I often feel sad and discouraged about my existence?

- Do I have the abilities and support to accomplish my goals?
- Why do my responses from others often make me feel useless?

The questions you may have struggled with answering, could be a sign that you should work on your faith. One of the easiest ways to work on faith is how we react when something gives us a challenge or hardship. When we are able to notice a hardship and make no reason to not complete it, we become steadfast in faith.

Another way to develop faith is to strengthen our respect for ourselves, which is more of the way we recognize and view ourselves. Improve our ***knowledge of self***, and we are more likely to uplift ourselves mentally.

Self-Respect

Self-Respect is the way we recognize or calculate our worth and is the ultimate belief that we place on ourselves. People who practice self-respect tend to be more satisfied with their true inner-self and exhibit a huge level of honor.

When we have self-respect, we admire our worth. People with no self-respect often stop themselves from doing something from revealing who they are because they fear that they would not be welcomed and loved for who they are.

Our fear of being appreciated often leads us to act in a way that's not aligned with what our heart wants because we want to feel welcomed and loved by others. To get over that fear, we want to let go of the requirement for approval from others. We could do so by taking time to be ourselves first, then we could demonstrate who we are without caring or feeling like others would appreciate us. Here are some examples of how we could know our self-respect:

- Do I acknowledge my qualities and skills?
- Am I always open for development and do I love myself as I am?
- Do I have to be valuable to another person?

The more questions that seemed challenging, the more you should work on self-respect. In order to grow in your self-respect, you can work on the following;

- Be your own best friend; use more time to develop yourself.
- Identify your skill set and accomplish something major in your life that pleases you.
- Love your own body; **your body is your own temple of God.**

Understanding ourselves often leads to better self-respect and more faith. There is also an aspect of connecting with self that's very prominent. The next chapter builds on that.

CONNECTING WITH SELF

Self is genuine, actual, and most of all truthful. We don't try to be someone we aren't or satisfy people we don't know. We sometimes know that we are unique but accept that reality of ourselves. For us, being different isn't an issue or something we seek to be ; we are just ourselves.

Our success comes from doing what's in our mind, what drives us, as opposed to what motivates others or the majority. The best way to connect with **Self** is to stop comparing ourselves with others. When we compare ourselves with others, we automatically feed a theory that we should be like others, seeing ourselves as not enough. This restricts us from being ourselves. Some of us often compare ourselves with others because we have the mentality that orders have it better than us. That could change into envy and resentment.

Take a minute to record all the things that makes you content and satisfy a space into your mind:

1.

2.

3.

4.

Now find ways to do more of this. A way to restore our true self is to regain our gifts and characteristics that we developed in school. Whether it's respect, fame, applause or acknowledgement, did we grow inside? We will always learn more about ourselves from the development from our school days to presently.

STUDY NATURE

Our first step is to pay attention to our outside nature; we can learn a lot from nature. What are the thoughts that cross our minds when we look or step outside? Do we see or think positively whenever we see animals, trees, the moon, or even the rain sometimes? What feelings do we recognize when we first feel rain or sunlight? Once we recognize the very nature of our environment, we can see that it aligns with the mindsets of us.

GROW OUR SELF-DISCIPLINE

Have we ever been out in public and noticed the immature mindsets of people? Does it make us feel uncomfortable at all? These people don't care about discipline. Discipline is the ability to acknowledge our inner state and develop ways to stay balanced. When we practice discipline, we are automatically allowing ourselves to be better forms of ourselves and don't allow our emotions to control us.

Being disciplined simply means that we can observe ourselves from an open-minded aspect. When we are disciplined, we catch ourselves in the current moment encountering a specific response.

The more we're disciplined of our emotions and behaviors, the more we start to know ourselves and excel into the mind of God. The ultimate reward of being disciplined is our ability to acknowledge when we are not in alignment with our true selves (***which is peace***). Discipline is the key to becoming a better version of ourselves and finding ***peace*** in all of us.

CONCLUSION

Being ourselves isn't an aspiration that we could all attain overnight. As human beings, we first have to accept that we are not perfect, and only strive for our eventual perfection. As you learned in this book, being the best form of ourselves isn't about perfection but more about finding our purpose.

Do not be afraid because of struggle; After difficulty comes ease. Do not hesitate to seek guidance from professionals or build a support network encouraging and inspiring you to elevate. No matter how bad the struggle, **You Got This;** affirm the best form of yourself today and forever! May peace be upon you.

CPSIA information can be obtained
at www.ICGtesting.com
Printed in the USA
LVHW090601070721
691973LV00003B/281